Hold my Hand

T0363180

PADDY FORSAYETH

First published in Far North Queensland, 2024 by Bowerbird Publishing

ISBN 978-0-6486041-6-7 (paperback)
ISBN 978-0-6486041-7-4 (hardcover)

Hold my Hand
Paddy Forsayeth

First edition: 2024

Illustrations by: Kai Hagberg
Edited by: Crystal Leonardi, Bowerbird Publishing
Cover Design by: Crystal Leonardi, Bowerbird Publishing
Interior Design by: Crystal Leonardi, Bowerbird Publishing

Distributed by Bowerbird Publishing
Available in National Library of Australia

Crystal Leonardi, Bowerbird Publishing
Julatten, Queensland, Australia
www.crystalleonardi.com

For many of us, there are times of disaster that are
confronting and distressing.

This compilation of poems resulted from my attempt to
resolve complex emotional issues over many years.

After my wife Maureen's death, a counsellor told me in my
distress that a day would come when my experiences could
enable me to offer some consolation to others.

I hope this little book will be a source of
comfort to someone in distress.

Preface

I was born in London, UK, a few days after the end of WW2.

I was the third child of Dr. Richard and Margaret Forsayeth. After a brief stay in South Africa, I, along with three sisters arrived in Atherton, North Queensland in 1952.

We lived for a while in an old farmhouse with no electricity and an active outdoor life. This lifestyle continued for most of my childhood, where my siblings and I would explore the world and do things independently.

Years later in Melbourne, I met my first wife, Pam, and after many weeks, we married in 1972.

In the seventies, I taught in a technical school which I enjoyed very much. Our son, Aaron, was born in 1974, and our daughter Cara was born in 1976. They were both delightful children.

Around 1982, I returned to teaching in Queensland. I eventually ended up in a small country school in Tara.

In 1991, our marriage broke up, which destroyed my life. My emotional incompetence stood in the way of reconciliation and retrieval of our marriage. I plunged into despair and depression. During this time, I went each week to Brisbane to see a psychiatrist who was very helpful in dealing with many emotional issues and my past life.

In 1993 I resigned from the Education department on the grounds of permanent disability because of my shattered emotional state.

In the nineties, during that terrible time, I wrote a lot of poetry dealing mainly with subconscious wounds and lost memories.

At the end of 1999, I arrived in Atherton to be with Maureen who I married in 2000.

After seventeen years of a wonderful marriage, my darling Maureen died from cancer. There is nothing that could have prepared me for that terrible loss, which I suffer to this day.

I hope that this book will help some of you who have entered that dark forest of despair.

Paddy Forsayeth

To contact Paddy, email racecompany@bigpond.com

Contents

Contents

My father was an English doctor and was not overtly affectionate to us children. However, he was kind and gentle. In my late teens, I thought about him and our relationship. One result of growing up in a large family with emotionally remote parents was that we learned to find out things for ourselves.

1

My Father

My father unwittingly did make
A bed of me when I was young.
And thereupon, as crumbs upon a lake
Did spread ideas from whence I'm sprung.

As moist soil which lies beneath the seed
Gives birth to acorns as much as weed.
For every flower as it turns towards the sun
There grows a reed.

But do not reeds enhance the flowers blush
And from blank ground, do not the colours rush?
Upon the ground that spawns a mighty tree
The grass grows lush.

And as an alchemer might still and bake and boil
Upon this clayey lot, he spent his toil.
But gold and silver he did not make of this,
He made it soil.

Some may claim the prize he might have got
Some may despise his only lot.
The tender care he laboured it with love
I've not forgot.

A potter might well enhance the clay,
And transform it – night to day.
And put it on a shelf for all to see.
'Twas not his way.

And one thing with hindsight I did learn,
That, though artfully he may have made an urn
I was not thrown in ambitions fire –
I did not burn.

Though earth has never caught the gardener's eye
Nor contemplated cloudy, stormy sky,
This little earth may grow some tree and weed;
Maybe, by and by.

Again, in my late teens, I was thinking about my relationship with my mother. She, like my father, was not openly affectionate, and this left me somewhat confused.

2

Of Cakes and Pies

When I sit down to breakfast,
Or lunch or dinner or tea;
There often lies a problem
Which many cannot see.
Should I eat of this or that,
Which one will I take?
Should I eat the apple pie
And leave till last the cake?

If at first I eat the pie
When my hungers keen
I often ponder on the cake
And the taste that might have been.
Would it be much better still
To leave the pie till last
Take first the cake and savour it
Before my hunger's past?

The problem here is not the choice
Between sweet pie and cake.
They are all the same to me
In either order that I take.
If pie and cake were people
What difference would it make?
If pie were chosen second,
Would its choiceness be at stake?

There are solutions to this plot,
Herein the answer lies,
I could abandon creamy cake
And forgo my apple pies.
But instead I satisfy
My stomach, pies and cake
By not appointing choices
In a resolution I did make.

When I sit down to eat a meal
This priority I do follow.
It may seem trite, it may seem light
But the reasons are not hollow.
When first I eat the apple pie
Its apple taste I savour.
And to last I leave the cake and anticipate its flavour.

In the year 1979, I was married and had two small children. I had joined the local rural fire brigade and rose in the ranks. There were times when the Victorian countryside was hot and dry and prone to bush fires. These were exciting times.

3

Turnout

The air is cool and breezy,
And promises one hot day:
The smell of heat is in the air,
The sun will have his say.

The cool already pressing,
The heat has come to stay:
Combustion there lies ready,
And will be here today.

"What will be the burn," one says
"The grass at Parson's Flat,
Or perhaps the Gorge with all its trees;
Or a house if it comes to that?"

Time drags on expectant,
The wind blows busily.
Dust and leaves are thrown aloft,
Down drops humidity.

And men in occupations
Are trying not to know,
That if the siren does sound off
They really want to go.

"You're all the same," the missus says,
"You half wish there was one!"
But when you're washing hoses
You wish it wasn't done.

When grief and desolation
Flay country with their curse
Firefighting has its moments —
Its excitement…and much worse.

Then Herman in his tower
Sights smoke on distant hill
You know you must be going,
As you feel a dreadful thrill.

"It's going up near Arthur's Creek,
It's going pretty strong!"
From sound and voice and urgency
You know he isn't wrong.

The siren wails its nasty song,
And up and up it grows.
You can be sure with anger
Hand in hand it goes.

The roar of pumps add fury
To flashing lights and bell.
The chorus of trucks' sirens
Add to this merry hell.

Turnout can be hectic,
There's little time to think,
But "Where's it at?" and "Who's on board?"
To mates we give a wink.

But when the truck is rolling
you get a breathing space,
to check the gear, to check the pumps;
to regiment your pace.

Sometimes someone will smell it first.
Before the smoke is seen ...
The odour of nostalgia,
Where gum leaves once had been.

Or then again you see the smoke,
Excitement builds anew.
Nervous smiles are passed around:
More so when you are new.

The heat is bad, but smoke is worse,
The stink of grass and gum.
And when you're dragging hoses,
You wish you'd never come.

In films there are heroics,
In grass fires there are none.
One hundred foot of canvas hose
Will weight a blood ton!

It's black and dirt and wet and muck,
No pats upon the shoulder.
And when the last grass tuft is out,
You're wiser, and feel older.

"Makeup!" the orders passed,
And that's a damned relief.
But you know when you get rolling,
The respite may be brief.

You're wet and tired, but willing
For you always know that when
The hooter goes, the siren blows
You'd be out there again.

I have a knack of telling jokes. This one was an experiment in language and rhyming.

4

The Shootout

The doors swing back, the doors swung hard,
In rolled the bastard, guns flashing in hand.
The nastiest critter you ever saw,
Swinging a new colt in his paw.
He lurched to the bar to make his stand
At the piano the player starred.

"A whiskey, bartender!" old deadeye cried,
As he shot some lead through the bar.
He guzzled the whiskey, blew lead through the floor.
And yelled to the barman to give him some more.
He stared round the drinkers, through he couldn't see far;
As he plugged the piano the player sighed.

The barman beckoned, and said with a smirk,
"Marty farn arns, the bayest evar seen!"
"Yark, shore!" (Blam! Blam!) the dude replied,
"Ah've threaten' hundrids, but none never tried!"
He blasted the ceiling, the barman turned green
The player smiled but kept on with his work.

"Now if ah wars yew," the barman said,
"Ah'd shore make that gern thane and smawl:
Ah'd gev it farl, Ah'd dep it in greeze –
Ah'd cut off them rough points, lark sheering' a fleeze;
Ah'd make it awl rounded an' smooth lark a bawl,
Ah'd make it awl sharny, lark a bawld jance head!"

The dude turned purple, and choked on his glass,
And waved his arms round in a menacing manner.
"Naowm wha werd Ah dew a fule thang lark that?"
The barman replied as he reached for his hat,
"When Wyatt Earp thar finishes playin' that pyanna,
He gonna sherve that gern erp yore arse!!!"

This poem is a reflection on the joy of being in love. I think this is a rumination of what love could or should be. In my youth and for many years I thought that love was an emotional infection, like getting the flu. I believed that if you had to work at being in love then you weren't really in love. It was only in later life that I came to understand what love is and requires.

5

If

If she were lovely as the day,
If she took his breath away,
If she really came to stay,
              He could love her.

If she stayed right by his side,
If she praised him when he tried,
If she held him when he cried,
              He would love her.

If she soothed his aches and pains,
If she cured his breaks and sprains,
If she whitewashed all his stains,
              He should love her.

And she's been here all these years,
And she's shared his joys and tears,
And she's soothed away those fears,
              He loves her...

In my early years I read a lot about the first and second world wars and came to appreciate the horror of those conflicts. In later years I came to realise that some men I knew suffered from PTSD, not recognised when I was young. The French village is Ypres but I remember my mother being amused by an Australian pronouncing the name as y-pers.

6

The Boozer at the Bar
(When Jonny went to Y-pers)

Johnny's just a boozer,
And he drinks the hours away.
All his mates like Johnny – or so they say.
But he's old, so very old;
And he's stuffed – or so they say.

Once Johnny was a young man,
But the cloudy days rolled in.
He signed up with all the rest,
And off to war he went.

His first taste was Gallipoli
He saw men burnt and bust:
But when Johnny went to Y-pers,
No one knew what Johnny saw.

The stinking fear and rotten queasy stench,
The lonely days of straining, waiting;
The bitter hours of killing, fighting.
To stay alive became his aim.

And hour by hour poor Johnny spent
His life, like water falling
When Johnny went from Y-pers
He was stuffed all right, he was

Some forget, maybe, and some remember,
Johnny could do neither right
So he drank to laugh and talk
With mates who'd been the same.

But that was sixty years ago, and still he drinks and boozes,
But even now old Johnny's forgot
He drinks now out of habit.
Yes, Johnny's forgot what Johnny saw
When Johnny went to Y-pers.

In 1991 my wife and I separated and this tore me apart. In hindsight I realised my ineptitude in resolving the marital issues confronting me. I am much wiser now and wish I had that wisdom then. This divorce utterly turned my life upside down. Many of the poems that follow were written as I went through therapy to explore my past and try to come to terms with the disaster I was going through.

7

For the Wife

Speak not to me of sin, for in its recollection
I am mindful of its weight.
And guilt and sorrow were companions
I knew well and intimately of late.
Thou wouldst not comprehend
How near to death I crept
Nor could thou imagine, now or then,
The rending tears of anguish that I wept.

For all contrition that I showed to thee
Could never penetrate that heart of scorn
And the tears of loss and terror
And the hopes of care were all false born.
Never was a soul devoid of pity, so utterly,
That in thy righteous bland indignity
Could turn so deaf to pleas and sighs
Unmindful of thine own complicity.

Didst thou forget my fidelity of years past
Was twenty years of marriage and support
So slight a thing that thou wouldst
Treat it with contempt – a worthless sort
Were thou so complacent in thy nest
And so fickle in thy professed love for me
When troubled winds disturbed thy rest
That thou didst gather up thy ragged care and flee?

What mean contract didst thou make with me
That always I should give and thou receive
That thou accepted all I gave in truth
That when I stumbled in my weakness
Thou couldst not believe?
How is it then that only thou canst know
The truth of things still hid from me
And in arrogance so twist your ears
To blight the words I put straight to thee?

A mighty gift it be for thou so blest,
To so divine the secrets in my heart
That before the breath of words had even passed my lips
Thine own ears had judged what they might impart
Didst thou only love me for my pocket
Was not my own standing fair enough for thee?

But blighted love must turn to dust I do suppose
And long indifference make it down to lie
In spite of innocent pretence and wrath
For all the good thou didst, it did but die.
I thank thee for the lessons thou has taught me
I thank thee for the bitter blows upon my body
I thank thee that thou didst break my heart and vex my soul
I thank thee for teaching me.

One of the great difficulties when going through this long and arduous mental and emotional trek was being unable to see the end or resolution. I was seeing a psychiatrist each week for nearly two years and I was teaching as this went on. My daily work routine was good for me but in my free time a lot of thinking, rumination and suffering went on. Writing this poetry was therapeutic and brought into focus the emotions I was exploring.

8

The Edge of Unknowing

I had passed through the forest
Unknown to me, and confusing
And I reached the side where all was arid.
Hot winds of despair threw up sands of bitterness
Which penetrated the crannies of my existence.
There being no landmarks I knew not
Where I was or who I might be.
It is a terrible land where you might die
There is no hope or consolation
Nor friends see in, but loved ones suspect
Those whom we love, would we take them there?

Hold my Hand

So dreadful there, where death sits
You meet him face to face
And he clutches and caresses,
He holds your heart and you feel
His deathly grip and you become fast friends
And eventually you know him well.
Yet he lets you be and waits
Like an old wolf sitting out the ebb of life.

He is in no hurry, nor am I
He is kind I guess; he does not take
He leads us beyond the desert; to where?
Who knows? Who cares? This much I know
That for those who cannot return to the forest
He at least leads out of the desert.
And some, needs be, must take his arm
To escape some painful misery.

He will submit to urgent pleas to rush
But know you that in your fear and pain
He is our dearest friend.
That poet, old Kyaam had said
To drink the wine of life but not to shrink
From the Dark Angel and his last sweet cup.

Now that I had met him and had spoken
About what might be and when
I knew he was indifferent to my passage
And I left, relieved and turned my face
Once more to the forest and confusion
And I knew that here I'd come again
One day and lean on his sure arm and take
The final road and bid him last farewell.

When one explores the inner soul and emotions there is much which is confronting and confusing. Sitting with the therapist and afterwards thinking about issues raised is difficult and at times a very arduous process. It took a long time for me to be able to sit with a memory or emotion and just let it be.

9

Desolation

And thus, the devils spoke,
one to the other
And wove the threads of human misery
To break the heart and snare the spirit
And break him on the anvil of mistrust;
To sap his strength with sadness
To blur his vision with anxiety
To foul his plans with panic
And thus, lead him to the black altar of despair,
To his ultimate extinction.
And always did they plot and scheme
The fate of broken destiny,
And laid the plan to lead his feet
From life and happiness to fear and death.
Lest he escape his evil fate,
Lest his agony be too short lived,
His confusion was assured

His pain was sufficiently intense
That he would struggle and ensnare
And trap himself beyond redemption.
And hence they shifted scenes on his life's horizon and on his map
To confuse his aims and debilitate his strength
So that in his struggles and his labours
He would work and never attain
That in his pilgrimage and journey
He would always travel and never arrive.
They numbed his senses and sensation
That in his seeking and direction
He would touch and never feel
He would look and never see and,
Even all attentive to the world around
He would listen and not hear.
To make him dumb and for confusion
He would talk and never speak
To break his heart and for unhappiness
Upon his ways they put about
Those sirens who would fix his ends
To despair his reality and realness
Thus, he would reach out and never touch
He would embrace and never hold.
And for his emptiness and fear
He would hold and never keep
And lest he falter and not endure
They planted there not love but cruel desire
So, he would love and never cherish.
And to fuel despair and discontent,
They proffered him his idol and mirage
That he would desire and not possess.
And when he hesitated at the brink
And to break his last despairing grip
They presented him with all the bits before
That he would know but never understand.

One of the disturbing things I found in this therapy was the exploration of an unknown past. This poem is purely speculative but the theme was one I was invited to think about. At one point in therapy, we explored the possibility of sexual interference but there was no memory at all of such a thing. It reflects my upbringing in which we children were not emotionally embraced and simply had to learn about life on our own. This had drawbacks and repercussions but also gave us fierce independence and the ability to learn on our own.

10

Growing Up

I grew up when I was three
I knew birth again from death and pain
I knew sex and slavery before I could speak
I saw passion in man's eye
I bore secrets I would never tell.

I grew up when I was four and five
I was old at six and seven
I grew up at night in dreams of terror
I lived on in spite of horror
I became my only guide and reason.

I held suffering as a secret
I was wedded to a covert guilt
I nursed hurt as a child and grew.
I was cut off from the love around me
I lived a secret life that none knew.

I reached out at times for love
But my little arms were far too short.
Love tried to enter my locked-up heart
But it was crowded out with pain
The closest thing I got was stimulation.

When I was ten, I stood apart and watched
I never took a thing that could be lost.
I became an expert in the art of love
I knew what it was not,
I learned to love from a far-off place

With skills and arts, I learned to compensate
I made my bridge to humans with my mind
I delighted them with jokes and stories
That they would love me and not hurt me
I was forever lost to feelings in my heart.

I cried to God, but where was he?
The Christians that I knew – the sons of love
Showed me the subtle ways of cruelty
Betrayed at three, of love's capacity bereft
I filled my aching wounds with learning.

At thirty I was already old and wise
Not of the world but of men and their desires
My imagination was a world where I was free
There I slayed my enemies with cruel designs
And I made love to them that none could see.

And now I take that ancient pain
And dissect it like the people I had seen
I take my shattered heart and soul
And rebuild them like they ought to be
A pain free edifice of true and simple beauty.

Do not tell this ancient man "Grow Up!"
I hung with Jesus on his cross
I wept blood with him in the garden
I rose with him on the third day
Jesus learned his words from such as me.

Cursed be he who adds pain to confusion
Blind is he who puts adults into children
A fool he is who reaches for the heart of a child
By putting his hand on her mind
Lost, yes lost is he who has no heart

Maturity is knowing the rules of adults
Growing up is connecting with the heart.
I grew up when I was but an infant
A lifetime thence I reached maturity
He was the man and I the boy.

To be attracted to someone when there is no hope of fulfillment is disappointing but something to be accepted. At about this time I began to examine my inner self and viewed that self as a little boy. In later poems he is called Billy.

11

Adieu

We let it go, that kite of love
We tried to hold it down,
Down here on earth
So we could possess it.
What a handsome kite,
A beautiful kite, so apt
So beautiful we made it;
And strong, yes strong
It rode the storms
It stood there in its glory.
No criticism could tarnish it
We made if for her.
She was beautiful as well
She deserved the kite
She never asked for it
She never knew, I couldn't tell
But we made it all the same.

See, we never had a kite
I didn't think we could do it
But what a beauty.
After many years we still held
The strings that bore us up in winds.
I often longed to show her
But it would have broke her heart;
I let go but the boy held on
This was the best kite he ever had.
And the lad was dragged along.
"Let it go son" I said
"This kite will never fly for her,
She will never admire it."
"Let the kite go my son
You will never fly to heaven
She dare not take it even if she

wanted."
One night we were playing
The kite dragged on a heavy wind.
"Let it go" I gently whispered
And he opened his little hands
And the beautiful kite blew away.
I think it went to heaven,
And the tears filled his eyes
They flowed down his cheeks.
How I hurt him, Dear God
And we cried and cried and cried.

This poem is a puzzle. It follows from the previous one in facing reality and accepting things as they are. There is no particular person that this poem is about.

12

Letting Go

What can I say about the war in my heart
The battles fought and never won
The strategy designed to bring defeat?
But I must walk again to nothing.
You are on the horizon disappearing
Your form becomes indistinct
You are small, a fragment of a dream
You have left me here, but you don't know.

I have buried you; I have put you away
The secret part of you is no more
You are gone but the love remains
Like the mist that hid you when you came
And hides your disappearing.
And like a mist it must succumb
To the warm heat of reality.

You were a wonderful and painful experience;
How many tears I wept in frustration
How often I smiled in true joy
How many times I breathed in awe
How countless the thoughts...

But now you're gone, almost
And I still see you, nearly
If I could reach out I could touch you, maybe.
I hold my arms in, I close my mouth
I have grieved for you who was never mine
I spoke words of love that returned unheard,
I wrote letters that were never sent
My love has shrunk to a warm affection
You made me grow, all unknowing.
You loved me without a gesture
You were but a vision
And the vision is nigh passed.

Again, when growing up emotionally alone one is forced to learn the ways of the world and the people in it. I stood back and observed and made many errors on my path to understanding other people. Exploring deep emotions at first is scary and confronting but with courage to enter that dark abyss and to patiently explore the pain is difficult but resolution and acceptance grows.

13

Trust

What child there be who, rudely thrust
Into the wasteland of despair and lovelessness
Gropes blindly for existence and true meaning
Who spies that faint glow and seeks
But in the seeking is moved by fear
That in the darkened distance by the shore
There lies the rocks to mark his end.

For are not sailors more craven still
When seeking land?
And many a ship lies foundered on the shore
Than on the deep?
How many lights stand out to warn of dangers
And by their very presence invite disaster?

We all need someone to communicate our feelings and inner emotions to. Only recently I have come to appreciate the benefits of being open with my moods and feelings with family and a few friends. The brave façade of denying negative feelings is firmly entrenched. With tact and frankness I am learning to communicate my emotional state to a few friends with improving benefits. I am also learning to listen with patience and empathy to others and myself as well!

14
The Light

You may never know what beacon
What faint winking light in storms
Your love is to him who struggles
Who rides the dark waves, is tossed.
Who roams with sight along the distance
Searching for that lighthouse on the shore.

In all the night your light will be
The only hopeful glow that he will see
And had you, unbeknowing moved away
Or even cruelly doused your light
He would now be foundered, shattered,
Lost……. Lost until he spies another lighted mark.

Hold my Hand

Let your light shine, let your love beam out
Unceasing, clear and strong
For the castaway alone upon the seas
Of the turmoil in his soul.
Let your love shine like a beacon
And hold him close if he comes home.

As I went through therapy, I had to do a lot of reading and reflection on the issues which came up with the psychiatrist. While logic is necessary for many processes there are some dilemmas and emotional black spots which defy logic and require feeling and emotions to come to grips with and hopefully solve and get through.

15

Working in Therapy

Sailor, sail the coast
Ride your sea
Hold your resolve
Like a rudder
Let hope be your sails:
Drive you on to different lands.

Throw reason overboard
It cannot guide you
To the land you seek
It has no heart, it cannot see.
Blind reason will never find
That light to draw your heart.

In the darkest night
When tempests set
Bind up your limbs
To the masthead of your resolution.
Lash your soul to the helm
And steer by love alone.

This is not only for the therapist but also for those close and supporting me.

16

For the Therapist

For always know that you may be
The only light that he will ever see.
And if you're filled with fear of storms
Avoiding dark and shapeless forms
And then you walk and take away the light
Who or what will guide him in the night?
Now you will need to stay long nights
And guide the darkness with remembered sights
Steadfast, strong, enduring to the end
Committed, all your care to lend
Never knowing if he could safely land
Or, when you reach, that he could even grasp your hand.
For you can always walk
Cast your candle in the sea
Return once more to haven,
Perhaps to flee
And batten down the windows 'gainst the sleet
And, not hearing, think the world complete.
How can he reach and knock upon your door
When he flounders, helpless far from shore?
How will you hear his cry upon the wind
And hear him tell how he has sinned?
How should he know where kindness lies
When your light lies hidden from his eyes?

I wrote these two poems in frustration with people, mainly work colleagues, who I felt were indifferent to my suffering. In hindsight I think my expectations were somewhat unrealistic.

17

Sects

Those silly sects and their silly sins
Where souls are sorted into bins
Where love is practiced in their heads
And love is absent from their beds
Where hearts throb in mirthless lust
And all end up in ash and dust.

The fools, when all is said and done
Beneath their joyless searing sun
What treasures have they stored poor souls
Filled they are with voids and holes.

18
Unfeeling

Of all good things I am filled
But none of them I share or give
Knock upon my door in vain
Cry out in your need and pain
Through I be filled with all good things
I cannot love so I can't give.

It took some time, years in fact, to appreciate that therapy and exploring inner emotions and memories requires a steadfast and brave endurance for all the pain, sorrow and progress.

19

Courage

What courage to endure
To pay so dearly
For undelivered and unknown goods.

What patience to wait
For times of peace
So far out of sight.

What strength to hold to life
Than to relax in huge fatigue
And slip into the arms of nothingness;

To curl up in the warm bosom
Of the universe
And sleep on into oblivion...
And painlessness.

At this time after many months of therapy, I began to observe a part of me which seemed to exist internally and somewhat separate from me. Later in life in similar circumstances I am reminded of the ability to look at negative emotions and pain with a degree of objectivity, which I find very helpful.

20

Encapsulated Pain

I lift the pain from its cot
I hold it in my arms
I love and care for it
Like a precious, broken child.

It reaches out with a dark finger
And drags its claw down my neck
It grins in childlike malevolence.
It would scratch my heart
As I look on its dark and scrawny body.

Dear child, where are you from?
Who spawned and birthed you?
No other one would love you
The way I do.
No other one will redeem you
The way I will.

Who will walk the path to crucifixion,
Who will weep and grieve for you?
Who is there whose tears
Will soften those prison bars
And allow you to go free.

Although you hurt like crazy hold on to me tight
So I in your painful experience become whole again
And you in the experience of my love
Will grow and smile again.

21

The Tragedy of Reason

Those cold old men
Who sit on the stark bench
Of their remorseless logic
And, bending to rules,
Think they practice love;

Who trade their bleak reasoning
Like some precious ware.
What would they buy then,
That is worth the sourness
Of their gall?

One of those lovely breaks in the long journey. Just a dream
I had.

22

Love and Sunset

My fingers clasp the petals lightly
A far-off gasp in air so slightly
A glistening stem so slightly shivered
A perfumed gem so full delivered
The blossoms sprightly touch the beams
Petals close tightly, returned to dreams.

I was undergoing therapy for Multiple Personality Disorder (MPD) and this brought up the notion of child identities, which I found difficult but helpful.

23

Nightmares

When the dark and hovered forms
Fill the sky and wings beat
When furry monsters climb the stairs
On silent furry feet.

When nameless terrors fill the heart
And reason's paralysed with fright
I gather round my children
And hold them in the night.

When I awake in shameless fear
And courage I have none
When I escape from dreams and such
And leave behind my sons.

I must look back and beckon them
And hold them in my arms
I stroke and soothe my frightened ones
With love and whispered charms.

I learned early to obey, to do what I was told. This acquiescence lasted all of my life. I am learning to resist and be myself.

24

Knocked Up

Why should I feel so guilty
Why should I feel so bad
Why should I feel so shameful
Because I suffered as a lad.

Why do I get so bloody tired
Why do I feel so coy
Why do I feel so listless
Just like a worn-out toy

I try to do my very best
But my best ain't very good
But I'll be brave and smile a lot
And do just what I should.

During the depths of therapy there was much explorations on deep inner feelings. Some of that was overt speculation which I had read from the literature that my therapist gave me. This poem is not real for me but mainly a topic and question. This has given me an understanding of the horrors and consequences of abuse.

25

Survivors and MPD

I survived Mum's boyfriend
He beat me black and blue
And when I told my Mummy
She said it wasn't true.

I survived my Daddy
I endured his frequent lust
When I cried out to Daddy
My Daddy said I must.

I survived the beltings
And all that awful stuff
But you should see inside my head.
That's where I'm really tough.

I've survived so many rapes
When my body wasn't mine
But ask me how I'm doing
I'll say I'm doing fine.

I survived some dreadful times
I walk around with pride
You cannot tell by looking
I'm all fried up inside.

I survived the beatings
I nearly came out whole
I survived the horrors
But I'm shattered in my soul.

I've survived that child abuse
And being burnt and hit
But like the chopped-up tree outside
I'm split and split and split.

In later years I have learned that the recovery is one that we undertake, that we provide the cure so to speak and the therapist provides the support and methods which we use to heal.

As part of my thoughts on the progress of therapy, this question came up.

26

Warrick

Oh, doctor can you mend my mind
And take away the pain
Can you close up all those splits inside
And make me whole again.

Ah doctor are you strong enough
To walk with me those years
And doctor do you care enough
To be covered with my tears.

Just out of the blue.

27
Who can Blame Them

Jesus Christ was lucky
He was crucified but once
My daddy crucifies me every night
Is that why I'm a dunce?

Jesus sure was lucky
He rose and went to heaven
I don't think that I can go
You see I'm only seven.

This is another speculative poem but it does hold some truth in that I had a personality who was separate and who embodied suffering. Dealing with Billy I found very helpful in uniting my feelings and personalities. The poem resulted from a nightmare I had of chasing a scrawny figure up a tall scaffolding and breaking its back. It also speaks about the difficulty in therapy of dealing with emotions which have little or no associated memories.

28

Meet Billy

I lie here in furnace heat
Burned I am from head to feet
I'll tell you all for what it's worth
I'll tell you then of hell on earth.

Remember in the dream you had
When you struggled hurting bad.
That was me, I cried and screamed
I was there the night you dreamed.

And when the going got too tough
With all the pain you'd had enough
You left me lying on that bed
You didn't stay, you went instead.

There's no blame for being weak
I don't begrudge the dawn you seek
The heat down here is far too strong
To hold you up as doing wrong.

And in the dream when round you went
In agony and double bent
With numbing blows and savage cuts
That's when he punched me in the guts.

That awesome nightmare when you ran
When you chased that cruel man
That's when the bastard in the sack
Bent me down and broke my back.

Then there's the dream in which I hide
When you lie face down in the tide
And endless peace where you are lying
And there was I in endless dying.

I'm the one who stayed instead
Who lay there in the rapist's bed
While you escaped and you were scared
And never knew and never cared.

Why do you think that I can't come
Why do you suppose I'm mute and dumb
I told you in the dreams you had
When you awoke and felt so bad.

I only speak in signs and pain
I can bring you hell again
But only when the night is filled
With silence and the voices stilled.

You think that you can walk right up
And ask of me please open up
But when I speak no words, you hear
And feel you then the pain and fear.

The only gifts I bring to you
Are stories what the bastards do
Expect from me no cheer and joy
I'm just a sad and broken boy.

But cursed I am, I'm only four
And I was treated like a whore
While worse and worser things they did
You ran away, you shit, you hid.

Delving into repressed painful memories was, and is, a difficult and confusing task. The poetic metaphor I used here was a good way to focus on underlying connection between the past and the present.

29

Dear Billy

I wondered why you wouldn't come
So, I'm the one whose really dumb
I didn't see, I never knew
I always thought that I was you.

It is true I ran away
To live and fight another day
If I'd have stayed upon that bed
I'm sure by now we'd both be dead.

And dead sometimes I'd like to be
And floating in an endless sea
Be born again, a brand-new boy
In a land filled up with love and joy.

When he was raped and he was torn
That's the time when we were born
I know you stayed like Isaac's lamb
While I went out and lived a sham.

But I've returned I've seen your face
In a far-off distant time and place
I hear your cries, I hear your screams
I hear you in my endless dreams.

Though I am cowed and filled with fright
I need your visit every night
Cos when you die then I will too
Then you'll be me and I'll be you.

Just out of the blue. This piece is simply a reassertion of the necessity to keep on exploring.

30

Searching

I must go back
Way out back
In that dreamtime place
Go back in time
Beyond that time
Before I knew that face

I must travel
And mists unravel
In that nightmare place
To see beyond
When I was fond
Of love and warming grace.

31

Puzzle

Is it night –
Or did the sun
Just go behind a cloud?

Is it you –
Or did I
Just speak my thought out loud?

I think this is more an internal conversation about keeping on with the therapeutic task at hand. As other poems have said going through painful and difficult memories and emotions is a trek to be taken one day at a time, one hill at a time...hold your hand.

32

Litany

Ask me not.
To leave the task undone,
Ask me not.
To drop my burden unfulfilled,
Ask me not.
To squander past regrets,
Ask me not.
To squander all the tears,
Ask me not.
To leave when just begun,
Ask me not.

Let me be.
If you cannot stand,
Let me be.
If your strength be less than mine,
Let me be.
If your will be unresolved,
Let me be.
If your faith be thin and bare,
Let me be.
If your heart be faint,
Then let me be.

Lift me up.
When I no longer see,
Lift me up.
When I no longer walk,
Lift me up.
When I fall upon my knees,
Lift me up
When I fall into despair,
Lift me up.
When I'm reaching up to heaven,
Then lift me up.

Hold me close.
When fear assails my soul,
Hold me close.
When desolation calls,
Hold me close.
When sadness fills my heart,
Hold me close.
When I awake in fright,
Hold me close.
When I come home again then
Hold me close.

One of those long-forgotten memories from childhood that came to me one day.

33

Do you Remember

Do you remember?
When your daddy held you close-
Do you remember?
The bristles on his chin
His rough caress
Those gigantic hands…..
Do you remember?
The rumbling in his chest,
His perspiration, his breathless embrace,
Do you remember?

I was thinking one day about the elusiveness of memories and the problems of searching for early experiences, how memories can be indistinct or not where you think you will find them.

34

Metamorphosis

I suppose they've all flown
From the place they've pupated
Away from the land
Where grubs are created

You go looking for grubs
All locked in their cases
They've all changed and flown
To far distant places.

Another poem about the difficulties of working and doing therapy at the same time. At this time, I was teaching full time and I got differing reactions from the staff to my condition, from sympathy to hostility. The theme is, again, about endurance and keeping on.

35

Getting Along Song
Sung to:
"She'll be Coming 'Round the Mouhntauin"

If the burden gets too heavy
Set it down
If the burden gets too heavy
Set it down
If the load is not set squarely
If it's loaded up unfairly
If your burden gets too heavy
Set it down.

If they treat you too unfairly
Don't bow down
If they treat you too unfairly
Don't bow down
Hold your rage just barely
And face the bastards squarely
If the treat you too unfairly
Don't bow down.

If you're feeling lonely
Hold your hand
If you're feeling lonely
Hold your hand
If you're feeling teary
And you're feeling weary
If you're feeling lonely
Hold your hand.

If the highway seems unending
Don't slow down
If the highway seems unending
Don't slow down
There'll be an end of sorrow
There'll be a new tomorrow
The highway has an ending
Don't slow down.

I could see in some of the staff their indifference to my situation and their impatience.

36

Guilt

When he breaks rank
And sits him down

He makes us shamed –
Us plodders.

Why can't he stand
And stager on
And hold us up –
The bugger.

My breakup from my wife in '91 precipitated the collapse of the world as I knew it.

37

Lament

Woman could you ever cross
Across the valley rifted
Seeing how we're far apart
And wide apart and drifted.

Thorny briars we should walk
And walk through thick and thin
To find lost love in broken hearts
The love that once had been.
And if you came, what would I know
What would I know to be
How faint the thread, the wispy thread
Binding you and me.

Woman would you ever care
Would you ever care to know
What this splintered soul, this amazing soul
Would ever care to show.

And always is your deeper loss
Not loss of me by sin
But loss denied of a child who cried
The child that cries within.

I have leapt from deepest sleep
Sleep shattered by your screaming
What devil's heat did your soul meet
What demon there in dreaming?
Ah woman did I tell you once
I told you once or twice
The heat is there beyond despair
And agony the price.

How little ever did you know
And know how long I'd be
How many days how many ways
I'd take in finding me.
Woman if you held my hand
And held your hand in mine
I would not dare I shouldn't care
To break your heart like mine.

Volunteers can brave their tears
Press on, though cowed with fright
I wouldn't take, nor you I'd make
A conscript in this fight.
And so perhaps a wiser thing
A wiser thing you did
To cut the tie, and dreams deny
And me a parting bid.

There never will a healing be
Though healing we will see
Of you maybe, perhaps of me
But not twixt thee and me.

At some stage I was doing some manual labour and this poem came up. By this time, I had come to terms with many issues and the poem shows some optimism.

38

Bloody Crowbars

You've never seen such sweatin'
Like a horse that's just been gettin'
A long and dusty gallop in the heat.
When a man picks up that bar
He'd like to be a star
Regardless of the summer and the hole.

With a force like jet propulsion
It has its own compulsion
To make you drive it, like a piston, in the ground.
You can spear a bloody toad
You can drive it through the road
Yep, a crowbar has a power of its own.

But when the hole is gettin' deeper
And the sides are gettin' steeper
Your enthusiasm wanes a bit you know
When your back is fairly achin'
And the biceps fairly breakin'
You'd swear you'd only had an inch to go.

Then the foreman on the job
With his sarcastic bloody gob
Comes and has a dekko down the 'crater'
"Upon me flamin' soul
I've never seen a hole
Go all the way to bloody China!"

And while the bastards' preachin'
Of all the blokes he's teachin'
How to drive a five-foot hole in solid rock
With your arse up to the sky
You bust your gut to try
To get the last damn bits of dirt by hand.

When its straight without a tilt
And the bar drops to the hilt
You reckon this one's big enough and deep
You can squat down on the ground
And have a look around
Take a breather and knock off for a spell.

Then when the job's complete
And the hole is clean and neat
Some smart arse will come and give advice
Though he's not a heifer's fart
He says (like he's real smart)
"Why doncha get a bloody auger, mate!"

In the background still the memory of recent therapy which had come to an end.

39

Childhood Lost
For all Those Abused Children

I hear the distant toll and roll
Of anguish like weeping in the night
Through the distant mist of memory.

The heavy veil of unremembered
Times so distant, out of sight,
Muffle the cries of those before.

A sigh perhaps and groans
Like the shuffling of tired armies
Walking at the dawn of time.

Though sounds be hushed the urgency
Speaks across the wall of now,
The cluttered presence of memories.

As if their upraised arms and hands
Were trees moved by the wind
The wind of their mindless pain.

And above and through it all
The hollowness, despairing, rings-
Abandoned, lost and hopeless.

I was back in the country and I was talking to a friend about refencing a property. This poem reflects the cyclic nature of things.

40

Fences

I know what you mean about a fence
A new one especially – it's got a twang
The strainers strong in their newness
The shiny wires glistening into the distance.

A new fence is assertive, proud even
Full of confidence, permanent, defiant –
Yet useful and compliant in a stern way
Yielding to a simple getting through.

But ages weary it; like us it sags
It yields again but to encroachment by weeds
And wattle and things that grow through it
And go through it, like cows and kangaroos.

The wires dull and even rust in places
And break and tangle, patched and torn
Posts grey with age and sun, and split
And eaten up by termites, and leaning too.

It turns from fence to barrier, impenetrable
Detours go around it not along it like before
It no longer stands defiant but succumbs
To the elements and the punishment of beasts.

Then a younger man will come and tear it down
And confine it to the tip; refuse, rubbish, mess
Plant new strainers, thread wire and barbs
Shiny and new again, strained up to a new day.

An observation on my life from one aspect. The early childhood was a time when I and my siblings had to work out what to do and how to do it, basically on our own. The mistakes we made, the accidents we made and the twists and turns we made in life tell the story of our maturing and reaching adulthood eventually.

41

The Moral of the Story

See the little bike his Dad give him? It's rooted
"Orf yer go son, into life on your little bike-the one I had."
See him travel on the highways of life,
one pedal goin' up an' down and the people laughin'.
The bent wheel woblin' to an fro,
weaving in the traffic, its bloody pathetic.
He will come to grief an' that's a fact.

The bloody handlebars
Loose in the forks, the steerin' shot to pieces, Jesus Christ!
The poor little bastard will stack it for sure.
Look at him –
Put his hand out to go right an' the bloody bike goes left
Just missed a dirty big truck; what a mess!

The old man orta been shot puttin' a kid on a bike Like that!
See the fat man ridin' the little bike his Dad give him
It's really sad, him ridin' along in the traffic pedallin' like mad
Arms an' knees stuck out weavin' all over the place
The handlebars not puttin' the bike where they should.
Its bloody dangerous!
See the poor bastard hit the kerb an' go flat on his face.
He orta have got the bike fixed or got a new one –
or somethink!
An' he shouldn't have been gawkin' at the sheilas
On the footpath.

See the poor old bastard lyin' in the gutter
He should have known
A bloke could have a bike that steered where you wanted
An' brakes that worked an' pulled you up on the spot
An' stopped you runnin' into things and getting' hurt.
It's pretty crook it took so long for him to learn a lesson.

See the poor bastard's missus; she didn't stop to lend a hand
She just kept up with the flow an' disappeared
Over the hill
An' she pinched his bloody suitcase orf the rack.

Bad luck the poor bastard got old and lost his concentration
The silly old fart reckoned she would stop and wait
Till he got back on
He didn't count on her pissin' orf and leavin' him
On his Pat Malone.

So, son, make sure you ride a bike with proper anchors
And one what steers straight an' doesn't wobble
An' keep yer eyes on the road and don't go gawkin'
At sheilas walking down the street flirtin' and stuff

And make sure the one yer ridin with is gunna stop
When yer get a flat or when the chain comes orf.
Otherwise, yer better orf goin' single —
On yer own.

42

A Beginning

There would never be a world
Where you and me
Would swim in our eyes
And mingle our mouths
In passion and tempest.

Would inhale the sensual,
The brush of lips on nose
The intimate fragrance
Of an ear or throat
Savoured and loved.

Where arms enfold, engulf
With willingness and desire
With the gasp of discovery
The openness to intimacy
Unimpaired by rules.

Another time standing outside the inner world of pain, one of those few times when I was relaxed and free from pain.

43

A Toast

Drink then! This good cup of port
Though it imparts intoxication
For all the while the angel's cup
With its pain still waits.

One day driving down to Brisbane I saw the train and pulled over to watch it. Again, another rare moment of peace and calm.

44

Dalby Cattle Train

I pulled over and raised the bonnet

To pretend to fix it
So, I could see her as she went by

So, I could hear her
As she rattled down the tracks.

45

Colleagues

You can see it in their eyes —
The pity: and they despise
The man who falters,
The man who cries.

I watched this elderly couple enter the Dalby RSL and mused about what sort of relationships people have, and about myself.

46

To Play the Pokies

She holds the umbrella
To shield the sun
From his head, his bald head.
He leans on the cane
His left leg wobbly rises
And steps and forward goes
The stick advances so does he,
The sun avoided by her hand.
And they walk; old and strong
Her hand is useless, it hovers.
His too, by his side
Does she still love him?
She still holds the green umbrella.
You wonder. Her hand hovers
Near his: he walks on the cane
She puts her hand in her pocket;
Is this the wife – stale in attention?
The hand secreted, no passion?
She attends, so caring, but
There is no life, just walking
Walking into the shade of the RSL
And the green tatty umbrella
Goes down and he is unaware.

I wrote this after my wife Maureen passed away. Maureen, a woman I adored and would do anything for.

47

Elegy

I never thought this day would come
To bring unseemly end
To happy days and holding hands,
The games and work we shared.

We built a life within our hearts
Like the garden that we grew
A life of joy and kindness
Our hearts entwined and shared.

I reflect upon this picture here
With you held in my arms
I look upon your gorgeous face
Your freckled arms, that smile.

Oh, what a joy it was for me
To live with you and share
The time we had together
So peaceful all the while.

But now that time is ended
But not my love for you
Our hearts entwined forever
Affectionate and true.
My darling Squidgems,
I will never forget,
I will never stop loving you….
me lovins!
Toj.

From the Publisher

'Hold my Hand' is not just a collection of poems; it is a compassionate companion that extends a reassuring hand to those in distress. I was left with renewed hope and understanding after reading Paddy's words.

I sincerely commend Paddy for seeking solace through his poetry after life's many tumultuous turns. This deeply personal journey forms the backdrop of 'Hold my Hand,' which explores various emotions including sadness, joy and reflection.

Congratulations, Paddy, on this stellar publication, I wish you all the best in your journey as a published author.

Crystal Leonardi
Bowerbird Publishing
Julatten, Qld, Australia

To order a copy of 'Hold my Hand' go to:
www.crystalleonardi.com/bookshop

Printed in the USA
CPSIA information can be obtained
at www.ICGtesting.com
LVHW090443161124
796806LV00035B/363